THE SIBLING THING

THE
SIBLING THING

How I Went from Prince to Pest
in Four Short Years

As Told to Saul Turteltaub
by Maxwell Lee Turteltaub, age 4

with astute comments by Ross, age 1

Tallfellow®Press

Published by
Tallfellow® Press, Inc.
1180 S. Beverly Drive
Los Angeles, CA 90035
www.Tallfellow.com

Designed by SunDried Penguin Design

ISBN: 1-931290-50-4

Printed in China
10 9 8 7 6 5 4 3 2 1

To my own loving and caring sibling, Helena Koenig,
who for all seventy years of my life
sibled better than anyone could hope for.

I am very grateful to Leonard Stern and Larry Sloan for their support in getting this book in publishable shape. Had it not been printed I would have lived the rest of my life in anguish, convinced that my younger grandson, Ross, hated me for writing a book, *The Grandfather Thing*, about his older sibling, Max, and none about him.

Table of Contents

Foreword

(by Grampa)

H aving written *The Grandfather Thing*, ("When you show pictures of your grandchildren to strangers in the next car at a stop sign, you have the Grandfather Thing"), I decided to write the sequel about that other phenomenon, the Grandmother Thing. The Grandmother Thing is turning down an invitation to dinner at the White House because there is a chance you might be needed to baby-sit for your grandchildren that night. When you leave your son's home at 6 p.m. while he is swinging your grandson over his head, and you are up all night waiting until 7 a.m. when you can call your son to make sure he didn't drop the baby, you've got the Grandmother Thing. When, in the hope of luring your grandchildren to your house, you buy a swing, slide, and tunnel set with a hundred parts and a thousand screws and nuts for your husband to put together even though he is still in a body cast from cutting a bagel, you have the Grandmother Thing.

I have found that a man generally does not get the Grandfather Thing until his grandchild is six months old or smiles at him, but a woman gets the Grandmother Thing at birth. Hers.

A woman is born with the ability to love funny-looking, creeping, crying, up-spitting people if they are directly related to her. Her early desire for a grandchild is made clear to her own one-day-old child when she tells him or her, "I can't wait for you to have a child of your own so you'll know what I went through to have you." Over the years this format will be used repeatedly: "I can't wait for you to have a child of your own so you can see how hard it is to bring one up." "I can't wait for you to have a child of your own so you'll know why I acted this way." And finally, "I can't wait for you to have a child of your own so you'll see I was right."

As a close observer, being the father of my wife's two children and the grandfather of her two grand-children, I can say with great conviction that a grandmother loves her grandchildren more than she loves her own children. This should not come as a surprise to anyone. The reason is clear: The grandchildren are never the enemy, and the children often were. She yelled at them, fought with them and punished them, all in moments of anger, frustration or disappointment. Naturally there was a good reason. They were driving her crazy, they were giving her a nervous breakdown, they were killing her and they didn't know she had only two hands. She was responsible for their lives, their mental and physical health, their food, clothing and transportation. Not a job any one person is cut out for.

But the grandchild offers none of those challenges. The grandchild is not her job. Someone else is responsible for doing all those things. The Grandmother, or Bubbe as she is called in our family, can pick the times and circumstances she wants to be with the child, and if the child becomes difficult, she can handle it with ease knowing it's not her fault or the grandchild's fault, but the fault of the parent—her own child—whom she always knew would never be as good a parent as she was and told him so when he was one day old.

The Grandmother Thing kicks into high gear when the daughter or son announces he or she is getting married. The first thing that comes to the grandmother's mind is not "I'm going to be a mother-in-law" but "I'm going to be a grandmother and the best grandmother any child ever had." With one announcement from our son Adam—"Rhea's pregnant!"—our daughter-in-law went from human being to jewel box. To her mother-in-law she was the container in which the Hope Baby was kept. A container that didn't know what to eat, how much to eat, when to eat and the equivalent "nots." Rhea was clearly a well-educated and informed woman who had studied all the right books and gone to all the right classes on baby-having, but she was not just having a baby, she was having A GRANDCHILD!

"The baby's going to be sickly, the baby's going to be too thin, it's going to have rickets. Rhea's not big enough, she should weigh more, she should eat more, but she shouldn't eat this, she shouldn't eat that. She should eat that and this and rest more."

At this point in writing *The Grandmother Thing*, I realized I could not finish this book without getting my daughter-in-law mad at my wife and me, which would be a terrible thing since she could deprive us of seeing our grandchildren and, as my wife puts it, "She is also the one who will be part of the decision to put us into a home." Humor based on truth stays humorous only until it hurts. Luckily, there was another story that began to unfold with more dramatic roots. Conflict at its highest. Brother against brother. Three years after he was born, Max, the amazing grandson, got a brother and *poof*, now there were SIBLINGS.

Siblinghood is an amazing relationship. People who are most closely related by blood are placed together in the same house and are expected for no good reason to love each other. The first siblings were Cain and Abel, and we all know how that turned out. While the oldest has the best of it from birth, being the only child and the sole beneficiary of all the attention and generosity of the parents, he has all of that to lose when the sibling arrives. As for the new sibling, he has nothing to be mad at yet. All existing siblings in the house at that time pose no greater threat than parents or furniture. They just come with the territory. Being a sibling myself, I am somewhat of an expert, having had two parents who each had siblings, and having fathered two sibling sons, one of whom now has sibling sons of his own. As an expert, I have learned there are no rules governing how siblings will act toward each other or feel about each other. My father had four sisters. He didn't talk to two of them and adored the other two. My mother had three sisters, all of whom got along nicely. My sister and I have always loved each other and gotten along, and my two sons never got along until they were in their twenties and have been best friends for the past twenty years.

How will Max get along with a sibling in the house? It's better if he tells you about it in his own words. I'm anxious to find out myself.

The Good Old Days

My name is Max. I was born in February, a little more than four years ago, with enough pounds and inches to be considered healthy. It took me two or three months to understand what talking was, and once I got it, it took another year for me to do it. By six months I understood everything everybody was saying to me and to each other. That's why, when I finally started talking at eighteen months, I just zipped through the language and started scoring big points with my family and friends.

They loved me before then of course. They thought I was cute when I smiled, laughed, clapped or hiccupped. They were not thrilled when I cried, but crying is how we talk. If we're hungry or wet and we laugh, we're not going to be fed or dried.

Aside from being overprotected, those early months were the greatest. I know now that better-tasting foods were out there, like ice cream and McChicken, and more interesting things to see (I could watch the garbage truck all day), but at the time everything was fine.

I was hugged and kissed by Mommy, Daddy, Pop Pop, Mom Mom, Bubbe and Grampa, and I got tons of presents. I was also hugged by the lady across the driveway who shouted to everybody how cute I was while she pinched me and threatened to eat me up. Who likes that!!! It was really a good thing that I couldn't talk, because there were times when I wasn't in the mood for hugging and kissing and pinching, and if I had said so I might have lost all those gifts! And since I was the only child in the family, I was THE PRINCE.

When I started talking at one and a half, I moved up to KING. Every one-syllable word got smiles, laughs or applause, and two syllables or the occasional miracle sentence had everyone running to the phones. Talking made life perfect. Before it, I liked what everyone did. After it, everyone did what I liked.

In the first three years of my life as far as my mommy and daddy were concerned, I did very little wrong. Once I threw my food off my tray and was told not to do it again, and I was smart enough not to do it again. Luckily they are the type of parents who believed if I didn't eat I wouldn't starve, and so they never made me eat when I didn't want to and they never got upset about it. And despite Bubbe's predictions, I didn't starve to death or get crickets.

I quickly grew into most of the outfits I was given at birth, and I looked fantastic as a baseball player and a sailor. At Halloween I was Blue, the television dog who happens to be a girl, but that didn't seem to bother anybody. However, the pea pod costume was no way to dress a King. As much as they loved me in my usual clothes, they seemed to love me even more in costumes.

They also didn't mind that I wasn't toilet trained at three. Someone or some book told them to wait until I was ready, and they waited patiently. I honestly could have made in the potty if I wanted to, but it would have slowed me down. The feeling always came up when I was someplace the potty wasn't, so I just did it without the potty, and luckily my parents were diaper trained and took care of everything. Shortly after I became three

I started getting funny faces from my next-door neighbor, Maya, who was younger than me. She'd say, "Oooohh, Max made. He smells." That's when I decided to commit to the potty, and everybody cheered.

I was very happy in my kingdom in the San Fernando Valley. Never yelled at or shushed. And then things started to change.

I had always been treated as the most important person in the house, but suddenly one day Mommy became the most important. Daddy kept asking her how she felt, what she wanted, and should she really be picking me up? What kind of question was that? She was the mother, I was the King.

I had no idea what was going on until I noticed Mommy's tummy getting big and everybody was touching it. Friends and relatives called all the time and came to the house and wanted to know if Mommy knew what "it" was going to be and when "it" was coming. She said she and Daddy didn't want to know what "it" was going to be, but "it" was coming in April.

I didn't like being left out, so I asked what was coming in April that they didn't want to know about. They told me Mommy had a baby in her stomach and when it came out it was going to be my brother or my sister, and it was going to love me as much as Mommy and Daddy do. How could they know that? They didn't even know what it was going to be. And how good could it be if they didn't want to know what it was?

How did a baby get into Mommy's stomach anyway? What did she eat? And what do we need it for? I don't need another kid in the house. If they wanted another person they should bring in Grampa. And where's it going to sleep? Not in *my* room! There's no space in my closet for it.

There Goes the Neighborhood

As soon as Mommy and Daddy told me I was going to have a brother or sister, they started telling me how much fun I was going to have playing with him or her. When he finally arrived, I could see *that* was a long way off. They named him Ross. This was a funny-looking person with no control of his arms, his legs or his head. Sisters probably look better. Couldn't look worse.

(Ross: And *you* were so beautiful? I've seen those pictures of you that Grampa took in the hospital when you were born. You looked like a chicken without feathers. The truth is, I was rounder and fuller and weighed more, which probably means I'll have more brains.)

I think it's better for me to have a brother than a sister because since I am a brother, I know what a brother thinks. Also, brothers turn into Daddies and sisters turn into Mommies, and I'd rather have another Daddy than another Mommy, since Daddies were little boys too and they'll understand me better.

(Ross: I can tell right now this kid is not going to be easy to live with.)

When Ross came home I could see it was very important to everybody that I loved him. If I looked at him they all said, "Look how Max loves his little brother." I'm sure they knew I was looking, not loving, but they were saying that to let me know it was a good thing to love my little brother, and if I wanted them to love me, I should love my little brother.

(Ross: He thinks too much. Lighten up, Max!)

For my sake I had to make-believe I loved my little brother. Really, what's to love?

(Ross: Plenty. The face alone is to die for. But more important, I happen to love Max. There's something cool about him. Like he's smart in a kid way and funny. He makes me smile.)

The truth is, I had no reason to love him yet.

(Ross: On second thought…)

I really didn't know what we needed him for. He's only trouble to me and everybody else in the house. He cries a lot. It doesn't keep me awake, but it does keep Mommy and Daddy away from me. When he cries they leave me and rush over to see why he's crying, and then hang out with him. Oh, they make sure I'm all right first, mainly because they don't want me to be jealous of him. That's the big new word in my life. Jealous. Everybody who came to the house only wanted to know if I was jealous. Actually *jealous* came later. First it was "Is Max J-E-A…?" Naturally, I had no idea what they were talking about, but the answer was always no, which seemed to please everybody. It wasn't until a few weeks later that I learned what jealous was. It was in my preschool class when Shira took a book from David. David had two books and Shira had none, and when David cried the teacher said Shira wasn't being mean, she was just jealous because he had two books and she didn't have any. Well, I don't know why these people in my house would think I was jealous of Ross, because he didn't have any books at all. The truth is, Ross should have been jealous of *me* because I had three years' worth of books and toys, and he just had a lot of clothes that didn't fit and a few toys only a baby would play with.

(Ross: The fact is, I didn't want anything anybody had. I just wanted something interesting to watch. The ceiling has only so much to offer. Those little hanging toys over my face were ok but Max was the best. He was always running around acting silly, and he'd stick his face over the rail of my crib and make faces at me.) Every once in a while, when Mommy and Daddy or my grandparents were watching, I'd stick my face into Ross's crib and smile at him. They thought that meant I loved him, and they would pick me up and hug and kiss me. But I was getting less and less of that since this kid came along. What kind of name is Ross anyway? Max is a real name. It sounds important, like what you would name a lion. But Ross? That's what you name a squirrel.

(Ross: See? He's getting testy. Picking on my name. He *is* a little J-E-A. And he should be. He had it all to himself until I came along. Like he says, he was the King. I can see now how it must have been. Mommy and Daddy are very nice parents. They carry on about everything he says and does. He doesn't seem much smarter to me than all those other kids who come over to play with him. They all talk the same and play the same. If anything, he laughs more than they do. Especially when they crash into a table or a wall and hurt themselves.)

As Ross got older, I started getting orders about how to behave around him. "Be careful." "Don't hug him too hard." "Don't throw the ball so close to him." "Be quiet, he's sleeping." And once, when I sneezed, "Don't bring your germs into his room." Like I sneezed on purpose. Why do you sneeze, anyway? I cough on purpose because something itches my throat, but a sneeze just comes out of nowhere. Before when I did it, it usually got a smile from the folks. Now it's trouble. This kind of thing really gets on your nerves.

(Ross: I'll tell you what gets on my nerves. Lying helplessly in bed with a huge brother in the house who wishes you were never born and who won't do time for smacking you in the head with Bob the Builder and his Bulldozer.)

My brother's first month in the house wasn't too bad. He did get his own room (where I couldn't bring my germs). But Mommy and Daddy were still concerned about me feeling left out. They were really into telling me and showing me how much they loved me and how important I was. I even heard Mommy say to someone on the phone, "If you're going to bring a present for Ross, bring one for Max, too." Then this: "It doesn't have to be expensive, just something so he won't feel slighted." That's how I ended up with twenty boxes of crayons. That was ok, though. I figured if Ross had never been born I wouldn't have gotten anything. By the way, Grampa taught me if I hold a bunch of crayons together in one hand and rub them across the paper I can make a rainbow. When Ross grows up I'll tell him it also works on the wall.

(Ross: What does he take me for, a fool? Even I know that's a time-out for life.)

Then I'll play hide-and-seek with him and show him all the good places he can hide in the house where nobody will ever find him, and how to splash all over Mommy when she's giving him a bath. I don't know why she gets so upset at being splashed anyway. It's bathtime, for crying out loud! If anybody should get upset, it's the person getting soap in his eyes during the hair wash. I'll tell Ross to aim for her eyes when he splashes her.

(Ross: I know he's out to get me, but this is all good stuff to know in case I get a baby brother or sister someday. From what I've learned so far, I think I'd like a sister.)

I wish I could write. I'd make a list of all the good

things and all the bad things I'm going to get out of Ross. For starters, they told me he'll be somebody for me to play with. That's a good thing. But he might be better at playing those things than me. That's a bad thing. I'm not very good at catching, and if he is then all I'll hear is "Watch how Ross catches the ball. See, Ross can catch it and he's three years younger than you." They don't have to say it in those words, but I'll know that's what they're thinking. I don't need to make a list after all. There's nothing he'll be good for.

(Ross: So shortsighted. He didn't think of it now but he will later. Everything he breaks when no one is looking, he'll blame on me. My only hope is Mommy and Daddy will put in one of those cameras like in the hospital, and they won't tell him about it. Ooh, look! I have toes.)

So Long,
Good Times

Today he's one month old.

(Ross: Happy Birthday to me, Happy Birthday to me. Happy Birthday dear Rossie, Happy Birthday to me!!!!)

To be perfectly honest it's no big deal.

(Ross: Awwwww!!!)

He looks the same and acts the same as he did the day he came home from the hospital. Maybe rounder. Come to think of it, he was round to begin with.

(Ross: Round is good. It makes rolling easier.)

Actually, he is the roundest kid I have ever seen. All of my friends are straight up and down, and so are Mommy, Daddy, Mom Mom, Pop Pop, Bubbe and Grampa. He looks a little like Winnie-the-Pooh. Maybe he's in the wrong family. Mommy should take him back to the hospital and find out, because if he doesn't belong here it's wrong to keep him.

(Ross: Wouldn't you love that? The fact is, I think I was better looking than all those other kids in the hospital. Less wrinkled. Younger, I guess.)

The first sign of my downfall came around this time. Ross was one month old. I was playing in my room with Grampa, who is a really funny guy, and he did his fake banging-his-nose-into-the-door trick, which always knocks me out. So I giggled and laughed, which I assume is what he was going for. Anyway, Mommy stuck her head into the room and in her loudest whisper—the one that's a little louder than talking out loud—she said without a smile, "Quiet, Max. Ross is sleeping." Wow. "Quiet, Max." I honestly think that was the first time in my whole life she ever called me by my name. I was always Sweetie, Honey or Sweet Pea. Now all of a sudden, I was "Max." And you have to believe me, that same laugh that I got yelled at for used to make her laugh and even give me a hug. Grampa, to his credit, quickly took the blame.

I really miss the old days. See, there was a bed in what's-his-name's room before he came, which I guess was for anybody extra who slept over, and it was the perfect jumping place for me. I used to jump on that bed and shout, "To infinity and beyond!" like Buzz Lightyear, until one day I bounced off, bumped into the window and was stupid enough to cry. That was the end of that. They took the bed out anyway when they put in Ross's crib. Too bad. I could have taught him how to jump and I'd leave the window open so he wouldn't bang into it.

There was no question; change was in the air.

(Ross: And it was spelled R-O-F-F!)

Out Cuted

I don't know why babies are born at no months old. They look and act the same as they do at two months. They cry and they don't play. I cried too, but there was a limit. Ross keeps crying even after he gets picked up. I don't know what he's going for. Picked up is still the best, even at my age.

(Ross: Well, it so happens I don't like being picked up. It's all right when it gets me to whatever I'm crying for, but in itself it's no thrill. I always end up facing the wrong direction.)

I think if parents are going to bring something into the house for themselves, they should also bring in something for you to play with so you won't be annoyed when the new thing is crying.

(Ross: Oh, man. J-E-L. He is Jellos.)

I did notice an improvement in his eyes. Now he was looking at me with both at once.

Bubbe and Grampa came over to baby-sit, and I saw a pattern forming. Grampa gave Ross a casual hello and then hung out with me the rest of the time, like he always did. But Bubbe gave *me* a casual hello—actually maybe a little more than casual—a big hug and a kiss, but that's it. She spends all her time with Ross. I've given this a lot of thought, and I don't think its because she likes him more than she likes me.

(Ross: I do. She likes me more. She thinks I'm cuter and smarter and rounder.)

I think it's because she's willing to do all the dirty work, like changing him and feeding him, and Grampa doesn't do that. Grampa likes sitting and watching TV with me. And sitting in the car with me when we go for drive. And taking me to the park and sitting. Sometimes he drives me to the baseball game for eating and sitting. When I was a little kid, both Daddy and Grampa would take me to the ballgame, and Daddy would carry me in and I didn't need a ticket. This year I learned I have to have a ticket, and since Grampa only has two season tickets, just he and I can go to the game. Well, what happens when one day Chubbo needs a ticket too?

(Ross: Go ahead. Keep it up. I may not be able to talk yet, but I can hear, and I will remember the name calling. Especially when I need a ticket. You think you hear me crying now? Wait till the playoffs.)

Actually, Uncle Jon has tickets, and he's more fun to go with than Grampa.

(Ross: Aw, heck!)

Wait a second. Uncle Jon may be the answer to my problems with El Bratto.

(Ross: El Bratto?)

Sure. I'll suck up to Uncle Jon and get to be his favorite. Ross doesn't know about all that yet.

(Ross: What, sucking? It's my specialty.)

And Uncle Jon will take me places and play with me and maybe Mommy and Daddy will start to miss me and send Ross home with Bubbe!

Well, two months went by and that didn't happen. At four months Ross started to smile. That did it. Everybody got hooked on him. The truth is, he did look cute when he smiled. And he smiled at me a lot. I liked that, because whenever Mommy and Daddy saw him smiling at me, they thought I had done something nice to him.

(Ross: Not likely.)

Not likely. Then it finally happened. The out-and-out yell. I can't believe I got yelled at. I threw a stuffed bear at him and shouted, "Catch, Rossie!" But that didn't fool anyone.

(Ross: Least of all me. What a shock. You look up, and there's a brown bear flying through the air right at your cute little face.)

I admit I really wanted to hit him with it, but I knew it wouldn't hurt him all that much. I wasn't out to hurt him, just bother him. Instead of going along with it, he cried. "Max!" they both screamed, the parents. While Mommy ran to pick up Ross, Daddy shouted, "That's a time-out!" A time-out is a punishment where I had to sit on the couch in the living room by myself and not talk to anyone and no one can talk to me. It used to be a big thing, but now it's not all that terrible. The yelling got to me though. This wasn't "yelling at me for my sake," like the time they both screamed "Max!" when I started walking into the driveway. I got scared and stopped right in my tracks, and they picked me up and told me how I could get hit by a car, and I knew they weren't mad at me; they were loving me. But this time it was different. This wasn't loving me. This was mad at me, and I didn't like it.

(Ross: Did you learn something? The whole rest of your life depends on how nice you are to me.)

There Go the Grandparents

Well, it was bound to happen. At five months, Ross got cute to everybody. Even Grampa. Before, Grampa never had a problem with ignoring him and just playing with me. Now he had to stop and pick up Ross and do all the things he used to do with me, like hold him way up in the air and then rub his belly over the top of his head. He can't do that with me anymore. He tells me I'm too heavy. I'm also too heavy for Bubbe to pick up and dance with, but Ross isn't. I jump up and down and say, "Me too, me too," knowing they can't but at least I can make them feel a little bad about it. (As if "Ring around the Rosie" is such a great thing anyway.) Then Bubbe whisks Ross away and Grampa plays baseball or watches TV with me. I like playing baseball with him better because he doesn't fall asleep during that.

(Ross: I'll play baseball with you when I get a little bigger. My rules. I hold the bat at all times.)

When Ross reached six months and I was three years and eight months, my life as I had come to know it was over. He was sitting up and standing a few seconds at a time and smiling at everybody for no reason at all. The family couldn't keep their eyes and hands off him. Come to think of it, I guess that was the reason he was smiling at them. The new kid was after my crown. He already had my clothes. I couldn't believe it. He showed up one morning in my Woody T-shirt. The scary thing was, I couldn't fit into that shirt until I was a year, and he was still in his months! And where did he sit? In my highchair. Doesn't this kid have anything of his own? Of course I don't need it anymore but at least ASK!!!!

I had to score bigtime with Mommy and Daddy. All I had going for me was my education. A three-and-a-half-year-old kid is only cute if there isn't a younger, cuter kid in the house. I knew my numbers. My counting was impressive, and I knew a few assorted dinnertime and Sabbath prayers that got their attention. I was also good at working the computer, TV, CD, DVD and cassette players. This continued to impress Bubbe and Grampa, who still can't set their car clocks, but Mommy and Daddy took it for granted. The only thing that could win them over was swimming. They wanted me to learn how to swim. Well, learning to swim isn't like learning to walk, count or anything else that isn't scary. The worst thing that can happen with walking is falling. But with swimming, you get water in your eyes and in your mouth, as I learned later. I was told not to swallow the water because it was dirty and had things in it that would make me sick. I asked why I had to learn to swim if it was going to make me sick, and they told me because I should know how to swim in case I ever fell into a pool. I didn't object to taking swimming lessons because Ross couldn't yet, and maybe I could be good at it and Mommy and Daddy would tell Ross I'm good at it and he can't even do it at all.

Anyway, my swim teacher wasn't very good and he didn't teach me how to swim. Mommy and Daddy didn't blame me though. I did my job. I got in the water, but I know there's more to it than hanging on to the teacher and crying. I'll get it sooner or later. Probably later.

(Ross: I was watching during the lesson, and I think if you take a deep breath, hold it, put your face in the water, kick your feet and move your arms, that should do it.)

The Handwriting on the Wall and the Ketchup on the Couch

As Balloon Boy approached seven months, I began to realize the way I was being treated wasn't all his fault.

(Ross: All right, Spinach. See, I can call names too.)

As I get older I just have more demands, and I haven't quite learned when not to make them, like when Mommy's cooking, when she's on the phone, reading the mail or feeding the kid. I like her to see what I can do. The somersault is my new big thing, but it has to be seen by somebody else. Why she gets annoyed at me for calling her to watch me and doesn't get upset at Ross when he eats is something else I don't understand. I eat with my fingers too, but he eats with his whole hand. And not from a plate, but from the highchair tray that the plate should be on. Mommy cuts up his food and puts it on the tray, and he picks it up with his whole hand and stuffs it in his mouth no matter what it is. And he mixes the meat with the vegetables and the tomato. And he misses his mouth a lot of times and it all just stays on his cheek until Mommy wipes it off and nobody cares, and I get yelled at if I drop a piece of lamb chop with ketchup on it while I'm playing pretend-airplane on the couch.

(Ross: I happen to like food. All of it and a lot of it. And I do feed myself. I don't drink out of Mommy anymore. I have a cup. Everybody still talks about how they used to have to follow you around with food in their hands, trying to feed you wherever you were hiding, playing or watching TV. No class.)

To be honest, I know that, while they have lost a lot of patience with me, they still love me. When I really feel ignored and not liked and I sulk, they notice right away and leave Little Vacuum Mouth to come over and pick me up and hug me. That still feels good. Sulking is a good thing.

Fighting for My Life

When Ross reached seven months I was really in trouble. He started to crawl. I don't know what took him so long. I think I crawled when I was one month old and ran up and down the stairs by the time I was seven months.

(Ross: You wish. Daddy said you didn't crawl until you were nine months, and then you only crawled backward. Weird.)

Now I'm supposed to watch out for him. If I step on him or accidentally jump on him, it's my fault. Why can't they just put him in his room and close the door so I can't hurt him and he won't bother me? I still don't get any fun out of him. He doesn't talk. I think when I was seventh months, I was saying everything.

(Ross: Oh, sure. Try paying attention. Mommy and Daddy said you didn't talk until you were eighteen months, and then all you could say was "Dada" and "Ma," which I guess I could say now, but then they'll expect a lot more from me and I really don't feel like doing that much work yet.)

As Ross started his eighth month, I got a chance to be a star again. Summertime was over and I was going back to preschool. I don't know why they call it preschool. It's school. I don't have my own room or my own toys there. I have a teacher and learn things I don't learn at home. Then when I come home and talk about the new things, Mommy and Daddy are very happy to hear. They tell me to tell Bubbe and Grampa when they come over, and then Bubbe and Grampa are very proud and make a fuss over me like in the old days before my baby BOTHER was born.

(Ross: Baby Bother? What a great joke! I'm impressed.)

Uh-oh.

(Ross: Now what?)

When I go back to school Ross is going to be here by himself with Mommy, Daddy and the nanny who comes in when Mommy and Daddy go to work.

(Ross: Oh boy.)

They're going to give him my toys to play with. He'll have it all. He'll be an only child from nine in the morning to one in the afternoon.

(Ross: That's right. So much for my morning nap. I can sleep when he comes home.)

As time goes by and Ross gets older, I've noticed something else that doesn't help me. I get older too. When I was a kid and couldn't talk and wanted something, I used to point at it and mumble some sound that sounded like it. No matter how mad I was that I couldn't have it or that they didn't understand me, they saw my pointing and mumbling as some sign of smarts, and they smiled and laughed at me. That's about where Ross is now. But now that I can talk and actually ask for what I want, they don't find it cute anymore. They either get it for me or they don't, and when they don't, well, naturally I have to shout at them and let them know how I feel about it. Without fail, this doesn't go over well, and it was during one such time that I heard Mommy call me a name.

(Ross: Well, it's about time you were at that end of the stick.)

"Pest," she called me.

(Ross: Yeah! And you deserved it. What does it mean?)

I had no idea what it meant, but I knew it wasn't good because as soon as she called me "pest," Daddy said, "That's it. That's a time-out. Go sit on the couch."

(Ross: Big deal. He sits on the couch all afternoon watching television anyway. Why not say, "That's it. Go sit on the couch WITHOUT YOUR BLANKET!" That would make him crazy. He doesn't have a backup. I have my thumb. He doesn't suck his thumb. Maybe when I get older I'll tell him about it. It's an amazing thing.)

So there I was, still in my threes and a pest. Over the next few weeks I figured out that a pest is a sweet little boy who bothers his parents about important things when they are busy, and then gets punished for no reason at all. I knew it was always going to be like this. Not only would I not be the King anymore, but unless Mommy had another baby in her tummy waiting to come out, Ross was going to become King forever.

(Ross: Yesssss!!!! That's me, King Forever!)

Unless…

(Ross: Uh-oh.)

…he becomes a bigger pest than me when he grows up.

(Ross: Not likely.)

There must be a way for me to make sure that happens.

(Ross: Oh, no. He'll do it, too. He's very smart. He knows how to fill the bathtub with water all by himself.)

We'll see. And I'd better get on it before he can talk.

(Ross: Da. Ma. Ba. I mean ball. I said Ba but I meant ball. Ba. Darn, did it again. ok, I'll work on it.)

Once he starts to talk I'll be able to say he said things he shouldn't, like "Dumb" and "Stupid" and "Shut up." And once he starts to walk I can tell Mommy and Daddy he did things he shouldn't, like touch the stove and go outside alone, and try to get into that mystery cabinet under the sink with the plastic lock on it, and make those marks on the wall in my bedroom that they haven't seen yet.

(Ross: Whoops. So maybe I don't have to be in such a hurry to say ball, or to learn to walk. The truth is, I can get the ball by pointing at it, and they carry me wherever I have to go. I'll just have to watch my weight.)

My Worst Birthday in My Whole Life

Today was my birthday. I became a full four-year-old and there was a big party for me.

(Ross: Yeah. I never got so many presents.)

Everybody brought presents and put them in the living room, and after they all went home, we opened them. ROSS GOT AS MANY PRESENTS AS I DID. That's right. I counted them. Up to five anyway. Remember all those cheapy boxes of crayons everybody brought me when he was born so I wouldn't feel bad? Well, you should have seen what they brought him on *my* birthday so *he* wouldn't feel bad. Just as good as what they brought me. Games and clothes and airplanes and bathtub stuff. How bad would he have felt if he didn't get anything anyway? He's only ten months old. A handful of Cheerios would have knocked him out.

(Ross: Wow, I'm ten months. I'll be a whole year in two years.)

What's going to happen at my next birthday party when I'm five? Are people going to say, "Let's bring a present for Max, too!!!!! Well, Ross's first birthday is in two months.

(Ross: Right. Months. That's what I meant.)

We'll see what happens then.

Happy Birthday, Rossie

So the big day came. He's one year old.

(Ross: Yes, I am. Wow. It's my birthday. I hope I get Cheerios.)

Nothing much happened to him when he turned one. I thought he would walk or talk on his birthday but he just stands up and sits down. Doesn't take a step. I don't know why he even bothers to stand up. Once I got behind him when he was standing and tried to help him walk. He fell and I fell on top of him. I don't do that anymore. As far as talking, I don't hear anything that sounds like it. "Ma" and "Da" for Mommy and Daddy is about it. He says "Gaaa," which Mommy says is "Max," but I don't think so. I'll ask him when he's three if "Gaaa" was "Max." If he can talk by three.

(Ross: "If he can talk by three." I'll show him. I won't wait until I'm three. I'll talk by whatever comes before three. A or B.)

Well, that night was his birthday party, and guess what? I got as many presents as he got, but there weren't all that many to begin with. I forgot he doesn't go to school yet and so he doesn't have any friends at all. There was just family at his birthday party, poor kid. I really got better presents than he did. We sang "Happy Birthday," but I'm sure he didn't have a clue as to what was going on. He kept looking at Mommy and she finally figured out he wanted his blanket. She got it for him and he fell asleep. He really looks cute when he falls asleep on his blanket with his thumb in his mouth. The truth is he looks cute when he's awake too. There's something about his wild hair and that all-out smile that says "fun." He may turn out to be a good buddy. Somebody to play with and he may even stick up for me when I get yelled at for being a pest.

(Ross: I will, I will. Hey, you're my brother. My big brother. Wow. I have a big brother. All right!)

Yeah. And from the way he looks now, I'll bet when he's all grown up he'll be strong and tough, and he'll be able to fight anybody that's mean to me.

(Ross: Yeah! What's "fight"?)

So you better watch what you say to me, Maya. Ross is my brother.

(Ross: Yeah! Who's Meyer?)

Looking Ahead

So, looking ahead, what's it going to be like having this little brother? I guess when we both get older and he goes to school, I'll be in charge of him. I'll make sure he doesn't fall off the monkey bars. I'll teach him to hide his leftover lunch in his cubby hole, and how to tie his sweater around his waist to cover up where he wet his pants. Those are things some kids do, I think. Then when he gets a lot older I'll probably have to drive him around in the car to all the places he has to go. How long does he have to use a car seat? How long do I have to use a car seat? Maybe until I'm as old as Mommy and Daddy. They don't have car seats. I guess that's because it's too hard to drive the car, work the radio and the CD, talk on the phone and eat in a car seat all at the same time.

I'll take good care of him though, so when we are both grown-up brothers like Daddy and Uncle Jon are, he'll like me and come over to my house to play with my little boy and throw him on the couch, and bring him lots of presents and tell him what a good little boy I was and what a great brother I was. And if he does that, I'll be his friend forever.

Afterword

(by Grampa)

Today Ross is twenty-two months old. He can walk, talk and defend himself. I take great pride in the fact that the first word he said was "Pa," referring to me. He was told I was Grampa just as Max was told, but Max called me Grampa from the beginning. Ross still calls me Pa even though he has mastered many two-syllable words, including "Daddy," "Mommy" and "Hello" (choosing to pronounce it "Huhwo" for reasons of his own).

I am still careful to give Max my primary attention because I don't want him to be jealous of Ross and angry with me. Somehow, I don't believe Ross will react the same way if I spent more time with Max. Besides, Ross is quite adept at communicating his needs. He'll let you know when he wants attention.

He starts by shouting "PA!" repeatedly, then he comes for me and pulls me in the direction he wants, finally hitting me on the leg for full attention.

Max seems to sense the younger-sibling-is-cuter thing, and as soon as someone takes out a camera he rushes over to Ross and begins hugging him. Apparently he has learned that's the best way to get in the picture. On their own they get along fine, generally ignoring each other. However, if Ross heads in the direction of trouble—an open door, a stove or a driveway—Max will quickly call an adult and bring it to his or her attention, clearly for the purpose of protecting his brother. There are momentary displays of sincere affection between them, and my guess is they will grow up as friends, or eventually become friends. No matter how they feel about each other, they will grow up being loved and seeing love in a house with loving, caring parents and occasional visits from the best four grandparents in the business.

Appendix

Famous Siblings

Some Got Along, Some Didn't

Cain and Abel
Cain was a farmer, Abel was a rancher. Cain gave
God a pile of vegetables as a gift and Abel gave
God steaks and chops. God naturally liked the
meat better, not having to worry about dieting,
and said so. Cain got jealous of his brother and
conked him with a rock.

Jacob and Esau
Twins. Esau was born first but for some reason
their mother liked Jacob better and so tricked
Isaac, their father, into making Jacob his number
one heir. Esau found out about it but let it go. Nice
guy.

Joseph and His Brothers
Again, a case of jealousy. Their father seemed to
like Joseph better than all of his brothers and gave
him a very fancy coat. That did it and the brothers
sold him to passing Arabs in the desert. Joseph
eventually forgave them all. Another nice guy.

The Kennedy Brothers
Joe, Jack, Bobby and Teddy. Devoted to their country, devoted to each other. Became famous as the brothers-in-law of Peter Lawford.

Orville and Wilbur Wright
Invented the first plane that flew. They got along well, although according to Red Buttons, they were up in the air for only fourteen seconds and Wilbur's luggage ended up in Cleveland.

The Andrews Sisters
Brilliant singing trio of the forties and fifties. Got along nicely despite the fact that they never knew which one of them was Maxine or Laverne.

The Smith Brothers
Made a great cough drop, but never stopped bickering. As a result, they were unsuccessful at finding the formula for their second invention, the sneeze drop.

The Van Dyke Brothers
Dick and Jerry. Good friends, although Jerry claims he made a mistake when he was born by choosing to be Jerry and not Dick.

The James Brothers
Jesse and Frank. Train robbers. Never got along because they both wanted to sit by the window.

Chang and Eng
Siamese twins. Inseparable.

Romulus and Remus
Twin brothers born in the B.C.s. Raised by wolves. Founders of Rome and Reme.

The Dionne Quintuplets
These five sisters were very close. That changed after they were born.

The Williams Sisters
Venus and Serena, tennis champions. Love-ing.

Shirley MacLaine and Warren Beatty
Loving brother and sister in this life. Who knows about the other lives?

The Lennon Sisters
Singing stars of the Lawrence Welk show. There was a one, and a two and a three of them.

The Baldwin Brothers
Alec and the ones who weren't married to Kim Basinger.

The Cassidy Brothers
Sean, David, Patrick and Hopalong.

The Carters
Jimmy and Billy. Jimmy was President,
Billy wasn't.

The Clintons
Bill and Roger, musicians.

The Jackson Five
Michael, Jermaine, Janet, Reggie and Stonewall.

The Marx Brothers
Groucho, Harpo, Chico, Zeppo and Gummo.
Nobody can remember their nicknames.

**And the Hills Brothers, who were up all night
inventing coffee.**